T0303659

More praise for *The First Church of What's Happening*

"Through these dexterously choreographed essays, Miah Jeffra perfects a grim exuberance that comes to suggest a new optimism. He writes: 'We made the Titanic, we made the Hindenburg, we made the Challenger Shuttle. We made Fukushima. We make love.' Certainly, the blood kinship of love and disaster—each here driven by human ambition for more self—animates this passage. But what deepens it is the breadth of Jeffra's 'we.' There is generosity here despite our capacities for self-righteousness, predation, and social inequity. I leave *The First Church of What's Happening* believing that what Jeffra evangelizes is resilience as a necessity, not a virtue."

– **DOUGLAS KEARNEY**, Whiting Award winner, author of *Patter, The Black Automaton* (2009) and *Fear, Some* (2006)

"A gem of an essay collection, shot through with humor, anger, and a deep, deep love—for men, for humanity, for language. In lush, risk-taking prose, Jeffra explores what it means to be queer, alive, and struggling in high-tech, low-empathy America. He takes the pulse of the now and quickens it with this sparkling debut."

– **JANET SARBANES**, author of *Army of One* (2008) and *The Protestor Has Been Released* (2017)

"Both tough and tender, sometimes laugh-out-loud funny and other times direly serious, Miah Jeffra flips the script in these essays on art, danger, seduction and sexuality. Moving between critical, narrative, lyrical modes Jeffra illuminates and entertains. I loved this book."

– **KAZIM ALI**, author of *Sky Ward* (2013) and
The Far Mosque (2005)

"Vision is a tricky enterprise. So writes Miah Jeffra in his sparkling new collection. In these lyrical essays Jeffra's quick eye catches what we often glide by, slide by, forget to notice, ignore. In these true to life, truer than life stories he shifts our focus from the obvious, the flash, the façade, to the subtle, background, underground, under skin tales where truer, deeper meaning resides. Luminous moments that often get less fanfare shine forth, rendered by a narrator who doesn't always shout look at me, me, me, but instead look at us, us, us. All of us; the fragile, the fallible, the lovely, the strange. This book not only expands our visual field but our intellectual, emotional and imaginative fields as well. Go see."

– **TONI MIROSEVICH**, author of *The Takeaway Bin* (2010) and
Pink Harvest (2007)

The First Church of What's Happening

Miah Jeffra

NOMADIC PRESS

OAKLAND

111 FAIRMOUNT AVENUE
OAKLAND, CA 94611

BROOKLYN

475 KENT AVENUE #302
BROOKLYN, NY 11249

WWW.NOMADICPRESS.ORG

MASTHEAD

FOUNDING AND MANAGING EDITOR
J. K. FOWLER

ASSOCIATE EDITOR
MICHAELA MULLIN

DESIGN
J. K. FOWLER

MISSION STATEMENT

Nomadic Press is a 501 (C)(3) not-for-profit organization that supports the works of emerging and established writers and artists. Through publications (including translations) and performances, Nomadic Press aims to build community among artists and across disciplines.

SUBMISSIONS

Nomadic Press wholeheartedly accepts unsolicited book manuscripts. To submit your work, please visit www.nomadicpress.org/submissions

DISTRIBUTION

Orders by trade bookstores and wholesalers:
Small Press Distribution,
1341 Seventh Street
Berkeley, CA 94701
spd@spdbooks.org
(510) 524-1668 / (800) 869-7553

The First Church of What's Happening

© 2017 by Miah Jeffra

This book was made possible by a loving community of chosen family and friends, old and new.

For author questions or to book a reading at your bookstore, university/school, or alternative establishment, please send an email to info@nomadicpress.org.

Cover and back artwork by Arthur Johnstone

Published by Nomadic Press, 111 Fairmount Avenue, Oakland, CA 94611

Third printing, 2019

Printed in the United States of America

LIBRARY OF CONGRESS CATALOGING-IN-PUBLICATION DATA

Jeffra, Miah, 1979 –
Title: *The First Church of What's Happening*
P. CM.
Summary: What does it mean to be American, Californian, queer, even creative, in an era of tweeted populism and hashtags? Miah Jeffra examines our new and rapidly changing public life by questioning a few fundamentals—perception, memory, identity, violence, love—in all their complexity, and in their relationship to one other. *The First Church of What's Happening* is a love letter to humanity and its resilience, even as it wades through divisive politics, social media and technological disassociation.

[1. ESSAYS. 2. QUEER STUDIES. 3.CALIFORNIA.] I. III. TITLE.

2017914842
ISBN: 978-0-9981348-9-5

The First Church of What's Happening

Miah Jeffra

NOMADIC
PRESS

for Kevin, and all those
who clip their wings

CONTENTS

17   GROWL

20   SUNSET, 2006 (THE MODERN
      PROMETHEUS, REPRISE)

23   MAKE SURE TO SEE THE
      EXIT DOOR

27   FIRST LOVE: A

30   HOW TO SEDUCE A TECH
      BRO IN 13 EASY STEPS

35   COFFEE SPILLED

38   TO AN EX LOVER, AFTER
      A NATURAL HISTORY OF THE
      SENSES

41   SUNSET, 1986 (I WANT
      TO TELL A STORY THAT IS
      TRUE)

46   LEAVING A MARK

49   THE STORY OF EVERY
      LIVING THING

"We fear violence less than our own feelings.
Personal, private, solitary pain is more terrifying
than what anyone else can inflict."

— JIM MORRISON

GROWL

THE RUMBLE COMES FROM deep in the throat, a low place, breath slow and soaked in the shaping of sound, a snarled pranayama, the chords fold and judder, their own capricious Ring of Fire. We never expect it. Our lips pull up in the way that we signal disgust, or mimic singing a Motley Crue song, our nostrils spread open in the scrunch, and the teeth, the canines, specifically, reveal themselves in the snarl. And the sound of gravel, of rumble, of some force coming. *Growl*. We can't even say the word without yielding effort, a full commitment of the mouth to convey the idea. A full, open-wide presence. *We are predators*, this sound speaks. But what does that mean?

My first memory of it is what one would expect: a dog. A hound. A long slate gray snout that juts from sagged eyes. A military housing playground in Norfolk, Virginia. I am six. I stand in front of the dog, this creature that appears so snug in the hub of civility, yet a beast. An animal. What makes this one different from the wolf or the bear? My six year-old genius suspects once peering into the dog, the mystery of this animal soon be discovered. I stare, committed to the science, my elliptical reflection in the black glass of its droopy eyes. And then it comes, the slow rising rumble, the quivering of slack lip, the teeth, and before I reason enough with my instincts to retreat, the whole mouth upon me, a soft bite, more of a warning than an attack. But the impression holds vivid, not so much the bite but the sound. *Don't fuck with me*, this growl says.

My mother's growl is wild and screeching and involves a frying pan in our trailer park kitchen. Her, in a bathrobe. Her second husband, my stepfather, in his threadbare underwear. The smell of eggs overcooking, garlic and farts. He swarms her with accusations that don't possess much specificity, that grow more abstract with their frequency: 'Where were you' and 'You should' and 'Answer me'. My mother's auburn hair crackles dry and electric, knotted on her head, some grabbing down her back and shoulders, Autumn straw sprung sideways, reaching out. Bill's litany grows more confident with my mother's silence, more cracking, more adolescent. "You, you, me, you, me, you, you, bitch, you, bitch, me, me, me" and then it emerges: the low rumble, grumble in the throat, the lips, the teeth, and then further, something even more, the rise into a shriek, high in the head and splayed out in three-dimensional space, a noxious sound. And the frying pan, from stove to my stepfather's shoulder, his mouth a big stupid O, my mother's mouth a rack of violence, eggs arcing through the air, steam on its rise off the fury and the food. *Don't fuck with me*, this growl says.

The growl of our stomachs. We hear it, and we think it tells us we hunger. In fact, that is not the case. Our stomachs, our intestines, ceaselessly serve to push, to send things from our mouths to our assholes. It is a loyal and perpetual labor. Smooth muscle contracts in waves, steers the stuff, perhaps fried eggs, through 25 feet of coil. It is always happening, every moment, but we only hear it when our guts are empty. That is when the sound reverberates from inside, suddenly played in an ampitheatre for its effort. It is then that we understand the want of the thing. It is an echo of need.

I am fucking a boy in Los Angeles, California. We are in the back seat of my car in the parking structure of Amoeba Records. I meet him in the used CD aisles, between Depeche Mode and Earth, Wind and Fire. It was in the middle of one of many slutty Hollywood interludes. A bell of sweat drops from my nose onto his barely there chest, smooth muscle, his tiny brown nipples, and then he makes the sound. The growl, teeth and all, eyes fixed. He is telling me, no warning me: I am an animal. You are a beast. We are all and only nature in this cramped capsule of pleather and plastic and metal and glass. It works. I get harder than I already am, yet am so hesitant of the hunger—so not as present, in my ambivalence—that I can only giggle, watching my body disappear and reappear into his own, this fleeting boy. *Fuck me*, this growl says.

Growls suppose an incivility. It is up there with ass-picking and hocking snot. We never expect it from ourselves. We *tsk tsk*, we denounce, we condemn its bestial origin, and yet our pupils come alive, a light in our moment, our bodies sweat, get wet, get hard, get sprung. What else does it remind us of? Are we not most beast when most immediate? Don't we always move from mouth to asshole? And isn't it us being our most civil selves, to give warning to our violence, before the bite, before the strike, before the demand to love?

There are people growling everywhere. At any given moment, there must be thousands of growls. A child in Yucaipa howls at her brother—that's *my* fruit-roll-up. *My precious*. A tow-truck driver in Oakland knows the roommate is gone, and the roommate's girlfriend has made it very clear that the coast is too with a condom in her teeth, a snarl of its own kind. Every day, there must be nurses, husbands, schoolchildren, baristas, carpenters, parking meter attendants, dog walkers, born-again Christians, vapor clerks that find their paws and claws, their rumble, in the folds of civility. Fathers alone must account for so many growls, the muddle of safeguard and violence so braided in their boyhood. And then there is Angela Cavallo, who lifts a 1964 Chevy Impala to save her teenage son, pinned underneath its metal and glass. Imagine *that growl*, that echo of need so strong it rattles in the chamber of every heart.

Every time a promise is taken, a promise needs shielding, a promise is about to be fulfilled. An about to, an about to. It's all in the about to happen that we erupt, these growls, these warnings of our immense power; how often, open-wide, we echo in need.

SUNSET, 2006 (THE MODERN PROMETHEUS, REPRISE)

I.

THE STORY OF FRANKENSTEIN is about a man and a monster. Man, shaped of clay, given fire. Monster, Man's puerile harness of that fire, an ugly shape. A metaphor that makes us: man and monster, lover and lyre, alchemy's folly, these thievings of fire.

This is what I told myself: all geniuses are broken children. A motherless boy bears the void, hardens desire, and chooses science: gives his entirety to what his grief believes. His clay self a bisque in the world while his soft stuff stays with its want; and within the wet center he whimpers. And from that, the brutal imagination.

Imagine the lightning. Plasma, forked and white against rain, the darker of nights. There is a lab coat, a stone floor. The scientist summons—no, that can't be. The scientist conjures—no, that can't be. The scientist *waits*, for the kiss of cloud to ground, a cathode crack in the indigo folds of cockcrow, and then the spark of life, more instinct than imagination. More meat than mind.

II.

You had such a hope in me, that I would kiss your cloud. I saw it in the way you crossed your feet when we argued. I saw it when you tried to parallel my steps when we walked. And the knowing of what failed was there, betrayed in the sight and the step. I'd blink, you'd blink. We would take the same picture, but always off by a breath, by our small hesitations.

There would be a dusk. You would stare into the falling sun, because you knew it was foolish, a disregard of body for beauty: the maker heart, the most adored of fools. You knew this, and I adored you, not because of this; you also loved the light, how it glinted your eyes, made you a different color. You would stare at the sun to find what you wanted in me, the blown shine smoothing my delineations, until there was only an open field for you to run through.

III.

The story of Frankenstein is about a man and what he makes. The child hides behind a curtain, and whispers instructions. Let's imagine, as you often do: on a slab, the scientist shaping matter, skin and bone, blood and coil, hand sculpting organ, heart, liver, lymph. Do details matter? He sees what he wants. He stares into the horror and sees a man, sees his mother, sees a promise, then another. And waits for lightning.

I told you that the story of Frankenstein was about a man who created a monster, and you said no it's not, it's about the monster himself, and I said that is a common misconception, and you said the commons were the people's progress, and I said I bet you didn't read the book, and you didn't say anything, and I said you just saw the Karloff movie, I bet, and you said that proves nothing. I didn't say anything. You said don't look at me that way. You said I was a misconception. You said there is truth in the skin of things.

Doesn't it only make sense that lightning would be the fire of life? Something to harness, the lust of it, something so unyielding, so violent. So not of bone, so not of clay.

IV.

Your hope was all around me, enveloping, manic, and I could have crushed you. The knees you made for me did not bend. The head you found for me did not bow. The heart you pressed did not beat your rhythm. I was afraid. You made me too big and I couldn't fit in the world. My hands squeezed, my feet thudded, my words stomped. I hurt everything, the soft stuff around you. I could not live as what you imagined; it was all large, and no multitude.

V.

The story of Frankenstein is about a man and what he mistakes. Isn't it strange that in some movie incarnations the monster kills his creator—isn't it a strange choice? Victor moves in to embrace the wretch, the skinned Adam of his labors (because we need to touch what we make, no matter how foul its form). And after its treachery, its plasma fury, its killing heart, killed, Victor leans into the mass, and a trust of no reason envelops him, and the creature envelops him, wraps giant arms, creation wrapping arms around creator (because don't we want the things we make to be bigger than ourselves?). And pulls the scientist into the experiment, snaps his bones, beaker glass beneath the weight of anxious fingers, that large hand to cowl, or small of back, the places where we fold easy. Isn't it a strange choice? Please know why I ask this.

Don't we all believe to bear it away? Don't we all stare into our want, relentlessly? Don't we all know the grief that burns a cottage to the ground?

I didn't want to be your monster. I didn't want the story of Frankenstein to be about you. But what is a story without want, anyway?

MAKE SURE TO SEE THE EXIT DOOR
for Keith Haring

DEAR KEITH:

I'm on Craigslist again. I am angry, ten years ago. And this is Hollywood.

The Casual Encounters ads are scrolling faster than usual; every few minutes a host of two dozen or so repopulate the interface, almost the same rate I am pounding plastic-bottle Gin gimlets, Nina Simone lamenting the whip of Parisian wind amidst the clanging AC of my dilapidated pseudo-Craftsman Hollywood cottage. The hot windless day broke open some rising need—in not only me, it seems; there is a flurry of M4Ms, of the typical photos—hairy chests and waxed chests, dangling and clenched dicks, finger-spread ass-cheeks and slightly parted lips filling the screen with overt sexual demands. I want to feel like a bandit, a punk, a renegade. Like you, Keith.

I first saw your artwork when I signed up for Best Buddies at a community service fair my Freshman year in college. Your work was the poster image for the organization: simple faceless figures—one yellow, one orange—arms over shoulder in that classic buddy embrace, against a flat blue backdrop. Best Buddies paired students with mentally disabled adults to go on outings in the community: the zoo, Six Flags. I always took mine—Bobby—to the Krispy Kreme and Kentucky Fried Chicken on Ponce De Leon Avenue in Atlanta. We would take our pink box and family bucket to Piedmont Park and eat it all, lick sugary glaze off fingers and chew cartilage from bone after I got stoned on my cheap eighth of shake. I think we had a good time, me and Bobby. I was probably breaking the Best Buddies rules. I'm sure you would have, too, Keith.

That Best Buddies poster always made me feel, what's the word, jubilant. Perhaps it was the short black lines emanating out from the figures, like vibrations, suggesting movement. Bursting joy? Adolescent jittering? Like ever some kind of possibility. The colors told me: this artist is resolute, satisfied in his bold strokes. Sorry, Keith. I was young.

I thought there was some kind of possibility with a senior named Kent, the other tenor in the University Singers chorale, who sat next to me, who tickled me during warm-up, the palest boy you could ever imagine. His thinning hair, the same color as his skin, resembled rough brushstrokes of a monochromatic portrait. He wore ripped jean shorts and no shoes, his feet cleft and mucky. His eyes bulged out, like a Boston Terrier's, lips swollen and cracked like a glazed donut. And, I loved him. I even told Bobby about him while I smoked my schwaggy weed in the park, about the time when Kent and I were alone in the auditorium hanging lights for a Christmas concert, and we discussed Judith Butler like we understood it, and he argued that Kinsey was right, and he kissed me and slipped his hands under my shirt, and we went back to his dormroom and I licked his fingers and we cuddled and fell asleep in each other's arms. My first hookup with a boy: a revelation.

Your animal drawings were always my favorite, Keith, especially the dogs, cats and chickens. I am an animal activist, too. Did you know that in order for a chicken to be certified "free-range", all it needs is a minimum of five minutes of access to the outside? At Polyface Farms—a certified "free-range" operation in Virginia—the "outdoors" comprises 5x10-feet fenced-in gravel pits available through a doggie door at the end of the coop, a space to share with no less than 1,000 other chickens.

Most Craiglist ad titles present a litany of raw tingling dangers: Lubed Ass in the Air, Waiting for Stud. I reply with a sepia-toned dick pic. Who Wants Their Cock Drained? Sure! Young Hung Straight Dick for Generous. BBC For Tight Asian Butt. Bear Wants to Train His Cub. I Wanna Drink Your Piss and Jizz. Glory-hole Cum Dump. Fuck Me While I Wear My Girlfriend's Panties. Let Me Lick Your Feet While You Take a Shit on My Mother's Glamour Shot Senior Prom Photograph. That one sounds punk rock. I click it; what do I get? A blurry cock flopped over the waistband of gym shorts. I reply with my body shot, flexing whatever little muscle I have. Another ad entreats, Are There Any Nice Men on Here Anymore? I skip. Cum on My Face? That sounds fun. I repeat with the sepia dick pic. I get a rather truncated response almost immediately: He asks me, "You a top?" I write, "sometimes." He asks me, "You masculine?" I write, "What does that mean?" He asks me, "Stats?" I write back that I prefer Analytical

Geometry. He ceases correspondence.

After my sleepover with Kent, I spent three weeks worth of nights on the grass of the residential quad, sitting under Kent's window, waiting until his light went out, hoping he'd glance out the window, spot me under the fluorescence with my face of yearning, that romantic Hollywood someplace-far-away face. But he never did. You see, he never acknowledged that night in his dorm-room, not even when we woke up the next morning, limbs and sweat, a tangled bed. He quietly pulled himself away from the naked embrace while I pretended to sleep, pulled on a pair of sweatpants, and began studying at his desk, his broad stretch of back shielding the rest of him from my waking. The back told me that I needed to go, and I slunk out. At the end of chorale practice the next day, I touched his shoulder; he spun and dared me. He whispered through his soft face, "I'm not like you. I want a family." Within 24 hours, he had a girlfriend. I wrote him poetry, would leave it in his mailbox.

I remember a first line of one of the poems: *What does it mean to be like me?*

I remember a last line of one of the poems: *I could love your paradox!*

I once told a guy at the end of a pleasant date that we could only make love for as long as a Nina Simone song. He asked me, "Who is that?" which is when I should have kicked him out. He asked me, "Why should we fuck so quickly?" He asked me, "Are you a top or bottom?" I said, "I like sex to be like a poem." He said, "poems are too hard to read." He said, "Men aren't supposed to be poetry." He asked me, "aren't you liberated?" I kicked him out. I sat under my window, and wondered if he was right. About the lyrical. About the liberated.

I didn't discover how you really felt about all of this binary bullshit until much later, Keith, when I saw your other images. It wasn't until I saw one in particular, of a headless body being strangled—not at the neck, but at the guts—all muscles and penis against a pink and glitter background—that I knew you were angry, after you had been checked in a bunch of recycled hetero boxes, after you had been rejected by countless lovers as too fem or too butch, too top or too bottom, too one way or the other, one or the other, apron or sledgehammer. How much liberation has there really been, that we still liken ourselves to Lucy and Ricky, to Ozzie and Harriet, to high heels and work boots?

Did you know, Keith, that even when the coop door opens for those "free-range" chickens at Polyface—that five-minute opportunity to splay their chicken feet on that wide-open gravel and take in the sunshine—they don't move? You would think they'd ache with the liberation, and scuttle towards the door, clucking loudly until that first sliver of light cracks at the bottom of their coop, feathers pouncing in that push to the great big liberty. But, no. The door opens and they sit there, stunned and still, clucking like fools. Even, now, after all these years.

I'm angry, Keith. I'm wound, just like your own strangled gut. Liberty is a poly-face.

I am certified, now, and this is San Francisco. I have rights. I can even get married. The door has opened and the crack of light is bright and glaring, and I get my five minutes of sunshine. But I want more than the five minutes anyone is offering. I don't want to be a certified free-range faggot. I want to roam the whole fucking farm. I want to wear the boots when I want, the apron when I want, to wield the sledgehammer while scuttling in the highest of heels, but more than that. I want none of it, so I can be *all* of it. I want to splay my feet on the grass of that college quad, only not looking up with a someplace-far-away face, but head-on. A renegade, against a flat blue backdrop. Because, like you knew, Keith, the only door worth walking through is the one to which you'll never return.

Ar•am (âr'ŭm). **1.** In the Old Testament, an ancient country of southwest Asia, roughly coextensive with present-day Syria. **2.** A common name among males in Armenia. **3.** In this case, lean and bronze, with amber eyes that pulled me into the horizon. **4.** I could never pronounce it correctly—only his mother could—but she liked me anyway, and allowed me to call him the Colorado River instead.

ar•bi•trar•y (är'bĭ-trĕr'ē) *adj.* **1.** Determined by chance, whim, or impulse, and not by necessity, reason, or principle. **2.** Based on or subject to individual judgment or preference: his choice to be a musician was arbitrary. **3.** Not limited by law; despotic.

SYNONYMS: arbitrary, capricious, whimsical. The central meaning shared by these adjectives is "determined by or arising from whim or caprice rather than judgment or reason": *an arbitrary decision; a capricious refusal; the butt of whimsical persecution.*

---

ar•bo•ri•za•tion (är'bŭr-ĭ-zā'shün) *n.* **1.** A branching, treelike shape or arrangement, as that of the dendrite of a nerve cell. **2.** The formation of a treelike shape or arrangement.

arc (ärk) *n.* **1.** Something shaped like a curve or an arch: *the vivid arc of a rainbow.* ~~**2.** *Mathematics.* A segment of a circle.~~ **3.** *Electricity.* A luminous discharge of current that is formed when a strong current jumps a gap in a circuit or between two electrodes. **4.** *Astronomy.* The apparent path of a celestial body as it rises above and falls below the horizon.

ar•cane (är-kān') *adj.* Known or understood only by a few. See Synonyms at mysterious.

ar•cha•ic (är-kā'ĭk) also **ar•cha•i•cal** (är-kā-ĭ-kül) adj. **1.** Of, relating to, or characteristic of a much earlier, often more primitive period: *an archaic bronze statuette.* **2.** No longer current or applicable; antiquated.

3. Of, relating to, or characteristic of words and language that were once common but are now used chiefly to suggest something that once was, but no longer: *I should have seen it coming.*

[paper, words, finite objects, and something always comes after.]

arch•ell (är-kël) *n.* **1.** The feeling of being betrayed, particularly in the condition of lustful advances toward those understood to be forbidden, by social qualm. **2.** I mean, totally off-limits cheating, and, certainly, with the kind of person that would evoke the deepest of breaks, the bone shard in the gut tissue, in order to demonstrate sexual power, superiority: *I'm beautiful, I'm beautiful, I'm beautiful dammit.*

ar•che•type (är'kĭ-tīp) *n.* **1.** An original model or type after which other similar things are patterned; a prototype: *"'Frankenstein'. . . 'Dracula' . . . 'Dr. Jekyll and Mr. Hyde' . . . the archetypes that have influenced all subsequent horror stories"* (*The New York Times*). **2.** An ideal example of a type; quintessence.

arc•tic (ärk'tĭk) *adj.* Extremely cold; frigid. See Synonyms at **cold.**

-ard or **-art** *suff.* One that habitually or excessively is in a specified condition or performs a specified action: *drunk-ard; cheat-ard; fuckt-ard.*

ar•du•ous (är'jû-ës) *adj.* **1.** Demanding great effort or labor; difficult: *"the arduous work of preparing a Dictionary of the English Language"* (Macauley). **2.** Testing severely   powers of   ; strenuous: a   , arduous, and exhausting
          . **3.** Hard to traverse,   , or surmount: *"you will never own me, Miah"* (Aram).

ar•e•ni•co•lous (ăr'ë-nĭk'ë-lës) *adj.*   , living, or burrowing in sand.

~~**ar•gue** (är'gyû) *v.* **1.** To put forth reasons for or against; debate. **2.** To attempt to prove by reasoning; maintain or contend. **3.** To persuade or influence (another), as by presenting reasons: *"I wanted to...but you wouldn't understand, not then"* (both of us, maybe).~~

ar•id (ăr'ĭd) *adj.* **2.** Lacking interest or feeling; lifeless and dull: *I would never give the satisfaction, not in words.*

[there are a lot of definitions, here. the precision, more security than the cup of a palm to face. I guess]

a•rise (ë-rīz) *intr.v.* **1.** To get up; as from a sitting or prone position; rise. **2.** To move upward; ascend. **3.** To come into being; originate: *hoped that new spirit of freedom was arising.* **4.** To result, issue, or proceed: *well, what else is there? Really. What else? Can one arise from a river?*

See Synonyms at **stem.**

[only pages believe the word truly lasts forever.]

HOW TO SEDUCE A TECH BRO IN
13 EASY STEPS

STEP 1. *SMILE*. EVERYONE would agree that a smiling person is far more approachable than a gloomy and surly one. Smile more often. It will make you seem easy going and happy, which will draw him to you. But don't overdo the smiling by making it obvious.

Step 2. *Sporadic Eye Contact*. If you don't want him to think that you are too attracted to him, relax on the little staring game. Look, but always look away just as he looks at you. By doing that, he will never be sure if you are staring at him, especially because in that corner coffee shop where you both are buying your fair trade pour-overs, he might think you're looking at another white male donning Warby Parkers and a messenger bag between the age of 25-32 whose name is also Bryan or Brad or Brent or Brock or Chett or Chip, but whose name would *never* be Cookie. When you use this little trick, a tech bro will start getting more and more curious about you.

Step 3. *Flirt With Him*. The best way to flirt is by asking questions. It appears more sincere. Perhaps you see his t-shirt that advertises his startup. Ask him what the app does, how it benefits all of humanity. If the words *evolve, progress or revolutionary* spill from his lips, you've got him. If all this fails, ask him about the hazing he had to endure in his fraternity. He'll dismiss this question at first with "It was just a way to make friends at Stanford," but really he is still a little embarrassed admitting that most of the workers at his job are Sigma Alpha Epsilons. Just make sure you follow up with your own frat horror story. You don't have one? Oh, you went to a state school? Well, make one up. But cease inquiry if his lip quivers, because that means he's not yet comfortable admitting to the after-party bro-jobs where he was "soooo fucked up" to remember.

Step 4. *A Little Peek-a-Boo*. It's always strategic to reveal yourself just enough to your tech bro. Wear shorts that cover, yet provide great suggestion of your ass. Brief engagement of visual repetition also goes a long way. We are creatures of myth, acolytes of serendipity. Seeing you at several of the same 15-minute 3,500 dollar junior one-bedroom open houses in the Mission adjacent to "bomb-ass burrito joints" and a Google Bus stop will get him thinking: *kismet*. And just before you leave, tell him you can make out the outline of his cock through his beige Chinos.

Step 5. On December 20, 2013, an unnamed dissenter hurled a rock at a Google bus in Oakland during a routine protest, shattered the window. Three of the passengers suffered cuts across their faces. *The Chronicle* determined this action to be the fever pitch of growing disparity between the rich and poor in the Bay Area. Karl Marx was quoted in the *SF Gate,* in response to the action: "only with great violence, comes change." As a result of the action, Google lost approximately 2,400.00 in work-hour productivity. All of the passengers eventually went to work. The bus window was fixed. No one quit their Google job. The protestors, part of the anarchist artist group Counterforce, claimed, "it's not personal. It's political." And, Jonah Wilson, a resident who witnessed the action, claimed, "Ain't nobody got time for that."

Step 6. *Unexpected Touches.* This is important if there is already mutual attraction. Lightly grazing his knee or his lexicon is key to sealing the deal. Mention API, GUI, BAP, CDMA, VC, especially because you're a woman and/or person of color that hasn't immigrated from East Asia, and he'll be surprised as much as impressed. Mention that you felt people were too harsh on Justin Keller, who was just voicing what all of us were thinking¬—I mean, why would any "wealthy working people" living in San Francisco want to see the "pain, struggle and despair of homeless people to and from their way to work every day"? Right?

Step 7. *Don't Throw Yourself at Him.* It's good to keep him guessing just a bit. Just as he tells you how his startup is changing the world, remind him that Dumpster, the app he designs informing when "friends" are taking a shit isn't really fostering interactivity in instances of need. When he tells you how his colleagues are the world's 21st century's artists, tell him that art is the conduit between humanity and the sublime, and that while a certain sublimation is involved in discussions of user experience, the irony does not escape you.

Step 8. I was in love with a boy named Chris, in high school. He was densely sandy-haired, full-lipped, big-eyed. He listened to REM and Operation Ivy and drew celestial figures across the grids of his Geometry notebook, organic loops betraying rigid lines. His ass filled a pair of shorts like two planets. We hung out in his room all night interpreting Tool's Psalm 69. He cried about our shared mortality over my lap and a bottle of Mad Dog. But when I leaned in to love him, to really love him with the length of me, he pushed away, denied the kiss and our history, left the circle we had drawn amidst the grid. With the silence came my fury. A week after the refusal, I keyed the body of his Honda and gutted his tires with a steak knife.

Step 9. *Sympathize With Him.* It must be so hard to be a tech bro, where everyone demonizes your existence. You're blamed for gentrification, for sterilizing formerly dynamic city-centers into consumer-driven cultural wastelands, for displacing blue-collar workers and artists. But this is a free market economy, right? Just because tech bros were clever enough to get themselves an education, work hard, and land a six-figure job doesn't mean they are required to buy art, or go to the theatre, or attend readings. This is Neoliberal America. Why blame them just because they prefer to spend their hard-earned money where they like—at bars with mint-flavored ice-cubes and restaurants with repurposed communal wood tables, and Cross-Fit classes? They have the right to spend their money wherever they want, right? The free-market economy is a virtue, like obeying your parents or neutering your pets. It's not tech-bros' fault that artists aren't clever enough to get people to buy their stuff. Maybe they should launch a Kickstarter. If they would just evolve or plug in to *progress*, then artists might not have such a bad go if it. Innovate or evaporate, dude. That's what Daniel Pink says. You know Daniel Pink? A real thinker, that Daniel Pink.

Step 10. Imagine the frustration of that protestor, the one who was so incensed by the rent hikes, by the displacement of the poor, by the white supremacy, by *Atlas Shrugging* all over Market Street, by the injustice, that upon sight of the rock's crude heft, the vulnerability of the thin glass, felt compelled to pick up and throw it, to exact harm somewhere. But where exactly? Anywhere more specific than merely beyond themself?

Step 11. *Ignore Him Just Enough To Want You More.* Allow for desire to bellow as you deflate the balloon of his own self-importance. Make him check and re-check his IM, fidgeting at the ergonomic desk in his favorite co-working space, called Würk, or Spæce. And when he asks why you haven't FaceTimed him before lunch, remind him that this is a free-market economy. Right? You can choose who to buy, and when.

Step 12. *Convince Him to Move to Wichita.* Or Providence. Why not? Why the fuck not? I mean, who needs place when we are all progressing towards an interconnected reality? Aren't we all the pages of *The Whole Earth Catalogue?*

Step 13. Think about Charlottesville. One group feels they have been disenfranchised by the self-righteous. The other group feels they need to quell the rise of a destructive force. Who is who? Well, perhaps that question illustrates a problem larger than either group attempts to resolve.

This list is obviously banking on you being angry, dear reader. Maybe you're nodding to some of these jabs at the tech bro. Maybe you're laughing out loud, thinking *snap!* Maybe you're even seething. Have you figured out why, yet?

Think about what lists do: how they whittle complexities to taglines, to Buzzfeed articles, to Twitter handles; how they whittle our integrity, how they carve us into singularity. How they take away our multitude. How they are born of refusal.

It's so much easier to exact fury on an individual than a complex, on a group than a system. Artists will tell you that our eyes require a focal point to locate within the entire field of vision. Activists are trained to know this. They could tell us this. The point? We want our shared mortality to be felt. That rock on the Google bus windshield insisted, "you will die too. Don't think you won't." But, to no one who could hear, not at that moment, anyway. The cracking of glass, the violence, was all that anybody heard.

Step 14. I know. The magazine you're reading promised thirteen, but there is always another and another, if we are walking nowhere. These steps are not dedicated travel. Progress is never a formula, and only fulfills itself when it's aware of what it affects. Where is the awareness in this? Say this to your tech bro. Say the word *formula*. Watch to see if his lip quivers.

Step 14 could also be: Don't throw rocks at Google buses. Or it could be: Listen to one another. Listen.

And that's the only step, really, to secure a tech bro, to secure a prom queen, to secure Peter in Finance, to secure the grumbling poet, the fixie rider, the hairdryer, the hordes of looking lovers; to secure anything akin to justice. Listen. You'll be surprised what that level of willingness and generosity reveals to you about us all.

And *smile*. Make it as obvious as you can.

COFFEE SPILLED

THE CAFÉ IS A worn, warm storefront on a stretch of street in the deep pocket of change, that used to be deemed unseemly with its whiff of raw fish heads and burnt pinto beans, with its car horns yelling across corners, with its hand-painted signs above doors, with its paint cracking, that used to be bedroom quiet in the darkest part of night, that used to be a haven for whispered drug deals. But now the drug deals are done inside, and the whispers are of lovers making deals, and the street narrowed, and our eyes widened.

The story goes like this: coffee spills. The woman who ordered the coffee is, by all accounts, lovely. She wears a sundress that drapes on her body modestly, but with terrific suggestion that her body is under this cotton floral print, and has the potential to do things. And now, the coffee that has spilled seeps into that cotton right on her breasts, where you now can see the outline of them, the bottom curve where they bulb on her chest. The coffee is very hot. Everyone in the café knows this because the woman, incongruous with her pixie haircut, her soft, round cheeks, her glossy pink lips, her linen lace-up Espadrilles, screeches out a nasty, nasally "Fuck!" She bends forward, pulls on the top of her dress. She says it again. "Fuck!" She looks wildly at the barista, a young man with a trimmed beard and a very thin, low-cut v-neck that flaunts his chest hair, this man who has stumbled against the counter and lost control of the freshly poured coffee that has spilled onto the pixie woman's sundress, and she says, "Fuck. You!"

There is another woman in the café. She is, to most, still considered young. Her daughter, with thin mousy brown hair identical to her mother's, sits across from her, and sees her mother's light blue eyes widen, watches her mother swing her head towards the pixie woman, who is still pulling the dress away from her chest in an awkward bend of her body. She says, "Excuse me. There is a child present." The daughter watches her mother's lips involuntarily tug towards her nose, and she might even call it a snarl, like that of a dog. Her mother was not a dog. She was usually calculated and muted, as if the animal instinct were rubbed out of her with sandpaper, and all that was left was a bone-smooth polish, her buffed fingernails reflecting little boxes of the window-light. The girl was too young to know of her mother's disappointments, all the lovers who had left, including her father, a schoolteacher who thought he wanted a child of his own—to practice his years of accrued insight—but who then realized he taught in a classroom because it was window-parenting, and that he more enjoyed a life that was outside looking in. The mother often envisions that the men leave because of the daughter, but then shakes her head violently to push the thought away. Yet it sits inside her, quietly breathing into the corners of whatever is left of her dreams. The mother packs up, rips out her keys, mumbling words like 'crass' and 'young' and 'bitch', leaps out of the chair, and says, "Come on, Sabrina," then glares at the pixie woman—whom she notices has awkwardly knelt down in front of her daughter—and storms out of the shop. Sabrina grabs her mother's half-drunk coffee and follows out the door. "Mom, you forgot your coffee."

The mother swings around, and pulls hard on Sabrina's arm, "Come on!" The coffee spills onto the sidewalk. The force of the anger, the energy that brews in the mother's body and releases in the seethe of the command, and the grip of the fingers on flesh, is so pointed, so specific, that it travels into the girl, red finger-wide bruises bloom under her skin. The shock of the energy, the pain of its force, goes through Sabrina, the look of her mother's fury superimposed onto her memory like the atomic bomb silhouettes blasted onto concrete walls. That memory will eclipse so many others, even of more profound events, and will reveal itself several times in her adulthood, most often as she makes love to men she has grown fond of, and worries they will leave. It is in the heaviness of sex that the memory will emerge, as if from deep water—the image of her mother's small tight face, the grit of her mouth, the grip of her hand—and with that Sabrina will transmit the force of the memory onto her lover—his face flushed, damp with sweat—through her fingernails, pressing deeper into his chest, and pulling down, until a small line of blood blooms from his skin, and his eyes open and widen with the instinct of terror. *Stay with me,* she thinks.

This is a story that we know, that we have read many times, and perhaps when we've read this story it transmits its force into us, and maybe we then carry it, and transmit it to something—or someone—else.

But there is another story here, the one that is less often written. It is where the young hairy-chested barista, once he has realized his mistake, that the bottom of the coffee cup has nicked the edge of the counter and the coffee sails into the air, once he sees the pixie woman clutching the stained cotton of her sundress, before her shock coalesces into the ball of fury that releases into that very audible "fuck", that he looks at her with so much sorrow, a blue cold that spreads out from his heart, across his chest, that wants to wrap itself around the pixie woman, to shroud her in the apology that could cool the red hot of the spilled liquid, and the white hot of her anger.

There is the moment where the pixie woman, after she has screamed her shock and anger in the form of that "fuck," after she turns to the angry mutterings of the mousy-haired mother and notices the 10 year-old daughter staring out, eyes widened, sees the innocence of the girl and recognizes her painful desire to preserve it, something identical to shame, that she lowers herself down, level to Sabrina and says, "I'm so sorry, honey," but this is only after the mother has already grabbed her and rushed out the door.

And that instant the mother sees how her fingers have violated her daughter's flesh, much the way her once rigid and now broken hopes have violated the precious little love that she still allows herself to feel, she becomes frightened for her daughter, the fear she will live in a world of little kindness, a world full of injury, and suddenly wraps her arms around Sabrina, picks her up with a strength that can only be summoned with the emotions of survival: either fear or love, but one can never see the difference in such small apertures, and Sabrina feels an instant of weightlessness, the burn of her mother's fingers forgotten in the cooling of her embrace.

And, finally, the tears of Sabrina, already falling as she punctures the lover's chest with her fingernails, the simultaneity of the anger and love raking his body, the urge to hurt and to hold, collapsed. And what of her lover? Which intent of hers does he understand first? Her fury, or her love? When his eyes widen in the violence, does he spread outward, or does he tighten into a hot white ball? And maybe, in this moment, Sabrina thinks *if only stories of forgiveness wrote themselves as urgently as stories of anger*. What would that mean for us all?

TO AN EX LOVER, AFTER *A NATURAL HISTORY OF THE SENSES*

WHEN I WAS SIXTEEN, I saw an alien. True story. My mama and I were watching television in our narrow low-rent Baltimore rowhouse when we heard our dog, barking with a particular urgency. Mama asks me to go investigate. I walk to the back, flip the floodlight switch and open the door. And there, at the end of our narrow concrete sliver of a yard, is Eggroll, looking up at a chest-high figure with an oblong luminescent face and large black eyes, staring directly at my smaller-than-average, teenage, presently and keenly vulnerable self. And immediately, without even a flash of hesitation, I shit my pants: a small, yet substantial, perfectly compacted brown nugget bullets from my butt-cheeks like a backfired slingshot. I could feel the velocity of that single turd shoot against the lining of my poly-cotton Voltron pajama bottoms, the betrayal of years of self-control, the pastel illustrations of *Once Upon a Potty* flashing into my mind's eye, as I waddled back to my mother with a face whiter than Ann Coulter. Ann Coulter. Wearing an eggshell bikini. On a foggy day. In a salt mine.

Vision is a tricky enterprise. All we truly perceive are configurations of shadows and light. True story. 127 million photoreceptors detect light stimulus, becoming electrical impulse along the optic nerve to the brain, and then a chemical, the mind, an open file without a name. And from this, we begin to make sense of our world.

My niece at nine months, beginning to crawl. One day I watched her amble directly into a piece of furniture, head-first. She thrusted with determined hands and knees, without hesitation, right into my sister's backless Wayfair barstool. Did little Mackenzie not see the metal legs? Why did she careen right into that pain, the boo-boo on her forehead? It appeared as if she hadn't seen the stool at all. *Shadows and light, electrical impulse, chemical, an open file.* And then, my sister, *mommy* to the rescue: She said, "Chair." Baby stare. "Chair." Baby stare. "Chair." Baby stare. Now, the open file has a name: language, a label, the sign.

Neurolinguist Richard Gregory argues that seeing is entirely hypothesis, reliant on experience and memory. We encounter a particular configuration of shadows and light, and that configuration is then matched to the closest file we have in our database. Your brain is a file clerk, searching for the match. Whatever matches closest is then pulled up and projected onto our mind's silver-screen. And that is what we see—not what we perceive, but what we see. Everyone knows a filing system is unsuccessful without explicit labeling. Labels are language. In essence, language becomes more our eyes, than our eyes.

Do you know the story of the Aztec genocide? The great, advanced civilization that initially and fatally opened its arms to Cortes' swords? They had a myth: The god of rebirth, Quetzalcoatl, promised to return one day from the East on a bed of clouds, to bestow upon the Aztecs the fortunes, the white hot heart, of the morning star. And then one day, in the dead middle of a millennium, upon the horizon, fishermen saw what they believed to be, approaching from the East, in billowing white, the promises of that morning star. See, the Aztecs were not sea-farers. And the billowing sails of Cortes' ships, well, the Aztecs didn't have a file for that, and those sails wound up becoming a different kind of promise.

And this is how you perceived me: a promise, a myth. I wonder what the story was that begat your creation of me. But I was not seen, that is certain; you were searching for a match. The language of the story you knew before you never knew me projected onto your mind's silver screen, before I even approached. And the Hollywood dream you thought you saw was all light and shadow, along the walls of a cave. And so you opened your heart, as if you hadn't even seen that I was only strong enough to conquer—not love—and you careened right into that pain. I am sorry for that.

If you haven't figured it out yet, I didn't really see an alien. I saw a possum on our back fence. The floodlight wasn't strong enough to pick up the chain-link at all, but it could reflect the rodent's iridescent fur on the top of its head, pointed down to keep a watchful eye on the threatening stance of my vicious Shih Tzu mix. The pose in illumination suggested the shape of that most common of mediated aliens—the bulbous head and sunken long face. My hypothesis was dead wrong. I didn't have a file in my database for something as odd as a possum on a fence in an inner-city Baltimore neighborhood. And, of course, what were my mama and I watching in the living room before the encounter? Mulder and Scully, forever engrossed in their sexually frustrated tete-a-tetes between science and magic. But in my mind's eye, in my memory, I still see that four-foot alien staring directly into my being as clear now as it was then, crystal enough to make me drop a stink pickle in my drawers.

When you don't collect much data, you don't have much in your database.

Recently, after watching a performance on YouTube, Ann Coulter called out Beyoncé for her salacious, female-demeaning lyrics, as an ironic parallel to the accusations of Trump's equally recent gender blitz. Ann tweets: Beyoncé, cited by Michelle Obama as role model for her daughters, sings about "pussy curvalicious, served delicious." Oh my. I just fainted". End tweet. Ann was probably promenading victorious at this burn, this apparent demonstrated hypocrisy of the smug liberal elite. However, what Ann didn't realize during that cock-sure strut in her proverbial pencil skirt, was that the woman she perceived mouthing those lyrics was not Beyoncé at all, but Nikki Minaj. Ann defended her mistake by saying, "they look so much alike."

  Black woman. Beyoncé. Black woman. Beyoncé. Black woman ...

  When you don't collect much data, you don't have much in your database.

  This tells me how we perceive one another: educated guesses, inaccurate file names, projected images, subservient to language. This tells me that if you were to see me clearly, you would have had to learn my language. Or, to learn a language beyond your own. Beyond the language of myth, and even beyond the language of billowing sails. This tells me that we all need to learn as much language as we can, to quit running into things that are there that we can't see. This tells me that if we commit to this—you and I, all of us—maybe then we will finally escape the shadows of the cave.

SUNSET, 1986
(I WANT TO TELL A STORY THAT IS TRUE)

My boy arms could be wings,
I was always sure of it.
My boy voice was an animal's,
whichever I liked.
All I wanted was not to be
the dark of men.

JACKIE ZLATER'S NEIGHBORHOOD PARK was my favorite spot for exactly the one year I lived in Quantico, Virginia. It had white wet sand (for building castles and stories of chivalrous journeys), a confusion of jungle-bars, and a large slide, all backing to a thick grouping of tall trees, the end of her community, the beginning of a children's beyond. Jackie and I called this the Magic Forest, and wandered through its springy bed of pine needles until we came to the other side, where a meadow of busy wildflowers grew for us to hide ourselves, play four-legged farm creatures beneath the blades, and make up more stories about princesses and goblins. The way the afternoon sunlight shone through the leaves and down onto the tree-beds made the forest colors alive, animated, like a scene from Wonderland, and not the edge of a military housing project. I had just turned 10 years old.

I used to catch fireflies when the sun warmed the earth hot and crickets sang their lust-songs. One summer night, however, while visiting my grandparents, my mother told me fireflies die when merely exposed to human flesh, somehow being harmed by the chemicals in our fingertips. The foreign poison brushes against them, and their life succumbs in a matter of hours. It horrified me that I possessed this poison, that so many people still caught them, knowing that they would die, knowing the danger of the touch. My mother told me this long ago, before she left—that space between this current story and then—precisely where my imagination became a thing beyond myself. On the day she left, her auburn hair frizzed from the salty Oahu air, she told me to be brave. I was seven years old, I was a shy child. She told me to be strong, to speak up for myself. At least, this is what my memory tells me. And for what?

My father and step-mother were fighting again—over money, my older brother's run-ins with trouble, my father's tendency to disappear—it all sounded the same in their voices. I snuck out the back door, as I often did, without them

41

noticing, as I often did, and across the housing project to the park. Maybe Jackie was there, but even if she wasn't it would be better than staying home. I didn't feel welcome in that home. Did my boy self know this, or is this an understanding as a man, as a writer?

He came from among the enchantment behind me. He may have greeted me. I knew who he was. I may have greeted him back. I was swinging absently from the monkey bars. At least, this is what my memory tells me.

And then we were walking in the woods. And then we were not walking anymore. And then his pants were down, and he was asking me to touch it. And I think I said no. I want to think I said no. I remember saying no. At least, that is what my memory tells me. It tells me that I began to walk away.

Which is why I remember the pressure of his hands, one around my mouth, one around my ribcage. The first thing: saliva from my open mouth seeping into his hand and smearing all over my nose and cheeks. I don't remember how I got to the crackle of the forest floor, but I do remember the thick whispering, "Shut up, shut up." I don't remember if I was crying here. Why do I even wonder? As he was fooling with my pants I stared, bewildered, up into the sky-break between the trees, black on blue, thinking the softness about the contrast of shadows nice. I perhaps even tried to pick up my neck to see it better. I know I would do that now.

I hate that I am a gay man telling this story. Any gay man can tell you why.

When I felt my bottom become exposed, I shot back to the moment, flailing my legs. His hands were pushing and punching all over my body, struggling to keep hold. With everything I had I screamed, shooting into the air, and it was answered by a horrible all-over pressure and a crack from somewhere inside my head. I suddenly saw blinks of light, and I imagined the fireflies were crowding around, screaming their light out in illuminating protest. That is the memory of my writer self, at least.

My own cries dulled to a distant, slow sound. I could taste blood inside my mouth, trickle down my throat. My eye felt pierced and hot, so I closed it in what I remember not to be fear then, but fear now.

He flipped me over onto my stomach too fast for me to move my face out of ground's way. Dirt and grainy nature stuck wet inside my slack lips, and I could feel the slobber move in my mouth. All I heard was his straggled breathing, a clinking and the familiar metallic friction of a zipper. He then lowered to my ears and grabbed my hair. His voice was quivering and unsteady. "Oh, God." He took a deep breath.

Did I say no? I definitely thought no. How fast it was, like the blink of light from the bottom of a bug. How ridiculous, a small word, yet the only one.

I once saw on a nature show what farmers do to pigs just before they are taken to be carved up. If I had seen that as a child, I never would have crawled on all fours and oinked to Jackie's bleating sheep.

An explosion of glass through my insides as the flesh tore close to my belly. I first became tense, a slingshot, all my muscles freezing up, then I felt nothing but muted weight, no sharpness, like my body was submerged in freezing water. I was drunk with pain, but only now could I articulate something like that. He quietly began to grunt as his hands pulled me apart.

I counted at some point. Six. Seven. Eight, my cheek scraping a twig. It was what I thought of. Numbers. My mind had been pushed out of me, and I became dumb, except for select things—counting, the loose collar button on my striped shirt, that hot dogs come from pigs (that's why they're killed), playing with Jackie Zlater. How much of that is what I truly remember, and what results in the writer colluding memory and meaning?

I don't think I was crying, just drifting without sense. His grunts had grown to high-pitched moans and they were growing faster and louder. His pushing became more forceful and frenzied. Then, in a most real and clear moment, I'm certain, he grabbed my shoulders from behind and pulled himself towards me. A new tearing. It felt like it hit something else, an organ, something else, my heart. I heaved forward and vomited.

He was finished. He pulled out, and shit and blood came after. He garbled something with a sneering sound, pushed me sideways, and stood up.

I opened my eyes for the first time since I was hit in the face, and saw him, with fuzzy light from the prolonged blindness. But I saw him clear enough. He was very dark, in silhouette, but I knew he was pale skinned, fair hair that appeared black now, dark shadowed face, light and dark. He was wearing the green camouflage common to the men of the barracks, at least that is what my memory tells me. But he probably wasn't. Perhaps that is a convenience for my story—not the one I write, but the one I remember.

The killing of pigs is simple, really. Farmers take a poker and pierce their intestines with a single maneuver. It's almost painless. Of course it makes sense why I mention this. I don't remember when I learned this information. It could have been after. Why do I loathe the smell of hot dogs to this day? There must be a reason. I'm sorry it slows the narrative down, but these hesitations are important in essay in a way they aren't in story.

I watched him with confusion and scorn, something between these. I already hated him, but at the moment was caught amused by how ridiculous he looked then, with his wrinkled thing hanging out and his face pruned to a whittled point. He jumped, fixed his clothes, rubbed his hands over his pants, looked unsure and lifeless at me, a dichotomous marriage of death and innocence—this I can say now—and ran, further into the woods. I imagined him running through the untamed bright beauty of the meadow, watching the long stems of the wildflowers wilt as he brushed past them with even the slightest touch, in his green and black, his pallid darkness. The face, only shadows, perhaps sorry and insecure, or confused, caked with despair, vague, but more than specific somehow. I listened to his muffled boots gradually diminuendo into silence until I sank, allowing the shock and exhaustion take me into a hard sleep.

And what did I dream during this sleep? I wish I knew. I could write that it was my mother, that auburn hair curtaining her face as she concentrated over a guitar on her knee. I could write that it was my mother, walking with me along an Oahu beach in a profound, mutual silence. I remember how often I missed her while I lived in Quantico with my father and stepmother, and I know that I could have dreamed about her while lying in the dirt and leaves. And that is why I include it here.

I woke to the accosting scent of excrement and dirt. The sun had fully fallen, and it was pitch. I pushed up to sit, and my butt and abdomen stung. With gritted teeth I pulled my jeans to my thighs, stopped, and rested. It was excruciating to move anything. This may be the most true part of the story, this memory. The left side of my face was swollen, bitten by the ground. I couldn't open up the eye anymore. There was a growing sharp throb in my gut that I foolishly concentrated on ignoring. After what may have been an hour, I stood up to my body's searing protests, carefully buttoned my pants, and looked down.

There was a slight imprint of my body in the ground, and the dented circles of his knees, bored deeper in the earth. I saw him again, large and looming, shadowed and sad. A small pool of red-brown mixed with acorns and leaves. Near the pool, pale amidst the murk, a single unmoving firefly. It must have gotten caught in the struggle and crushed under my weight. I lowered my finger to its abdomen, now lightless, and poked, even though I knew it was dead. At least, this is what my memory tells me. The boy? The man? The writer? They are all characters here, sometimes indistinguishable, sometimes reflective of one another, sometimes at odds.

I walked home, careful, noiseless. I had to walk with my legs spread apart as much as I could, to avoid the friction. It must've been funny to see my little figure, alone in the fresh night, shaped like an inverted "Y". I didn't care about what I looked like, or about how I was going to clean up. And I wish I could admit that I only thought of this man's pitiful, sorry boyness, awkward with the darkness of his adultness, or that I thought of *my* boyness, and became afraid then of what I would be, what all men become. The writer does, for sure. I hate that I am a gay man writing this story.

I can believe that I thought about my mother again. I know thoughts of her eventually became so strong that, soon after, we reunited, after three years. And somehow in all the years that came after, I remember never feeling anger that she had left me, at all.

But if I listen to my memory as a boy, I think it was the simple, primitive sounds—the grunts, cries, cracks—and the firefly, that were in my mind as I walked home that evening. The nature, and us. I feel sure of it, writing this.

My mother told me to speak up. I try to write what I know, but I can never be sure. This is more about me, now, than me, then. You know this.

What should I have thought of as I walked home that evening? My father noticing me like this? I don't think that ever occurred to me, because—at least what I recall as a man—he rarely noticed me, anyway, and never found out. My mother leaving? This would lend the story a layer, because—at least what I recall as a writer—there is a connection in these two pains.

I want to tell a story that is true.

But if I tell the story as a boy, I thought of the sounds and the bug. That is what stayed with me, all the way home, a looping reel, never leaving the arch of my eardrum, with more precision than the act itself. Of all things. I heard the sounds, I thought of the firefly. I thought of the firefly; I wanted to go to sleep.

LEAVING A MARK
after Felix Gonzalez-Torres

THERE IS A BILLBOARD. A white bed, rumpled white sheets, and white pillows, in a white room. The pillows have deep hollows, impressions, where a heavy head would lay in its comfort. But the bed is empty. White.

"Is that an ad for fancy sheets," asks a fellow student. We are in a shabby corner of 90's Brooklyn, on a high-school field trip, going somewhere, I forget. This is all I remember about any of this trip, except for the Spring New York air, the urine and the black tar tang of the river brack, of a climb into the crown of Liberty herself.

I can't stop staring at the image. I feel its loss. I somehow know the people who aren't there, without ever seeing them. It is a false knowing. I am 16.

Felix Gonzalez-Torres created this billboard to honor his lover, Ross Laycock, who died of AIDS-related complications. He said of his work, "Above all else, it is about leaving a mark that I existed: I was here. I was hungry. I was defeated. I was happy. I was sad. I was in love. I was afraid. I was hopeful. I had an idea." Felix died four years later, from "AIDS-related complications".

In the gay community we have our first stories, like any other: first kiss, first love, our 'first time', but we have others ones, too: our coming out, our second 'first time', our first hate crime, and our first death from AIDS. Mine was Michael, who lived across the hall in my college dorm, who came over at three in the morning to ask if he could cuddle, just cuddle, nothing more. Who had smelly hobbit feet. Who went to class donning an apron that said, "Kiss Me. I'm Irish." Who wrote me unrequited love poems and left them on my empty pillow. Scrubby fuzz on his chin, gap-teethed, grinning, when he drank gin in a plastic flask, urging to us all the virtues of pure democracy. Five years later he was found dead in his hotel room in Washington DC. Working as an aide for a Georgia state senator's campaign. His body lay in the middle of the king, legs together, arms at his side, little plastic baggies, a spoon, a rolled up twenty. He had been diagnosed three weeks before. It was the 90's. We thought AIDS was a death sentence, and Michael decided to finish the line himself.

My generation was that in-between: after the education and before the hesitant sigh of relief, before Atripla and Videx and Emtriva and Zerit and Ziagen and Retrovir, before PREP and Truvida and ARV. We had condoms and celebrities, PSAs and polished hair. And the word death. Death. In pink helvetica. In essence, we were terrified to have sex. But we were alive. We were safe. We did everything safe. I prided myself on doing everything safe.

My roommate, Irwan, is also of my generation. He went to art school—a writer, a painter. Then, he stopped. Now, he cooks. Rice, spicy noodles, curries that tear away the tops of the tongue, and meat. Lots of meat. Busies his hands. Hums to himself to block out other noises.

He didn't want to know. Whatever the virus was cooking in his guts, he pretended wasn't there, the hiss inside, in his ears. He sang louder, in clubs with their bass thicker than the blood he never tested, in squealing bars, in cloudy porn shoot bedrooms. Then, another image, an abacus of him dying, six T-cells, 98 pounds, two weeks to live, a countdown, beads sliding along string, a litany of Latin syllables mapped over his body, his throat, his skin, his stomach waging war with the hiss that folded out of sound and into a breath heavier than any sex he ever had. In the generation before us, Irwan was supposed to die. But he didn't.

Torres created many works about the absence of his lover. One was a giant pile of Hershey Kisses, in the corner of the gallery, the glinting silver chocolate bulbs, Ross' favorite, each glint a cue in the dint. The viewer was instructed to take. Eat. Then toss the wrapper in another pile, a smaller one. Little silver scraps. Rubbed to tiny balls by the pointed fingers of those very much alive.

>
> Dear Felix,
>
> > Now, in the ground, then, on the bed, which
> > were you walked on the more?

Irwan quit making art after his diagnosis. That is, save one work. A small painting, on wood, the top of a pill box, in a hospital pink background, with the first letters of each day, one on each flap: M, T, W, T, F, S, S. The hiss. I wondered with indignation why he quit making art. I feel the answer lies in this last painting, somewhere, in the names of days. I stare at the little boxes with their letters, planned, filled with pills, his life. His only way to life. A different kind of death.

Michael's head pressed the hotel bed's pillow, did it not? With no lover next to him. Imagine the photograph. A bed. A pillow. A billboard never made. Is it easier to know the impression of two? Is it more painful to see the hollow of one? One without the other makes the one alone, unknown. Is that the hiss?

The pillbox. It tells me. Art has changed. The reminder is not the loss, but that we now are alive. What of this difference? Pillow to pillbox, death to some kind of life. Can art leave a mark on behalf of lives not gone, but unseen? Is that where the suffering lives on? An AIDS-related complication.

I did everything safe. I am healthy. I have pride. I have been in the crown of Liberty herself. And the view from there is lonely. I crawl onto my bed and impress my whole body, pitch my head, dig in deep. My false knowing. I have pointed the finger, many times. And the finger that points forgets that the only thing true is the finger itself.

THE STORY OF EVERY LIVING THING

STRUCTURES—BIG *THINGS*—ARE making me panic lately. Large, beyond-the-size-of-human things that we dwell in, that we swarm inside, that we rely on to stay intact. Made by us. Every time I bike or drive or walk over the Golden Gate Bridge, I can't help but marvel how this 80-year-old thing stands in the water so confidently. Why doesn't this crashing wild water erode the foundation to the point of collapse? I ask this to my roommate, Sean, who prides himself on his physics knowledge, even though he is a photographer for hipster hoodrats in the Lower Haight. We are driving over the Golden Gate with our friend Marie to get Dippin' Dots in Sausalito.

Well, eventually it will fall. I mean, it *is* water, he says.

Exactly, I say. Look at what it does to earth, to metal, to skin.

Nothing is indestructable, he says.

Then, why do we drive on this thing?

Why are you asking this while we are on the bridge, Marie asks.

The bartender at The Page and a tremor (un)plant the idea. I am sipping my Pilsner, the hiccup of earth occurs, and debris from the ceiling dusts the floor. I look up. Everything looks the same. Large brick slabs nestle between lines of concrete mortar. I look at her, and she's shaking her head. I share the empirical probability that if shakes like this happen enough, the ceiling could fall—*the sky is falling, the sky is falling*. She laughs, and then stops laughing. Wow, that's deep, she says.

Why? I ask. Her eyes stay fixed on the ceiling.

It ends, man. You know? It ends with the nothingness that, like, when the whatever that was whatever has finally ceased, you know, being what it was, and becomes many things, or many parts of things. Or maybe it's nothing at all. You want another beer?

I stare at the ceiling with her.

It begins with the observations, quick glimpses, interstitial musings that bob now and then, when the air isn't too hot or cold, when the spaces between our doings aren't busy swatting away bugs from our face, yelling at drivers who cut us off, pushing ourselves into the world with a force that could never be mistaken as listening. A woman is talking on her cell phone during her lunch break. Her panini sits patiently as she pulls a strand of loose hair, fiddles and releases it into the wind. The hair dances nervously, snakes in its weightlessness, then settles on the back of a chair filled with a man who is talking on his cell phone during his lunch break. He doesn't have much hair left. But he does pull on his nose. He smears the crusty mucous, some on his creased slacks, some on the edge of the table. He misses his mother, who passed away the previous September. He is considered attractive by several people. So is the woman. She has already forgotten about her strand of hair, but it has only begun.

In the bathroom after school. I am burning paper because it is punk rock. Trying to convince Chris Curtis that we were supposed to join our bodies in splendid oneness, I watched the fire pare the white paper into gray ash, then fall, disappear out of sight, wondering where it went. Where was this nothingness and suchness?

I was watching the mini-series adaptation of *Angels in America* (I had read the play, and loved it immensely, more than the mini-series, but then is *not* when I got a boner, and that is what this is about). The actor playing Louis says to the actor playing Mormon Joe that smelling something is the particles of the object coming into you. The object—that very real thing—sloughs off bits of itself at all moments, every moment, a little bit and a little bit. Upon hearing this I get an astonishing boner.

Making out with Karen Fiorito in the 10th grade, I unexpectedly got a nose bleed. She didn't care, even laughed, while my tongue was licking the back of her teeth. Afterwards, after the wetness had dried on her skin and panties, she recoiled at the thin brown line down her neck. I touched it. Where it was dry, it rubbed off and disappeared.

My father opens his hands and says nothing when I ask him why he is my father, why I am his son, the vastness of the question in my small five year-old mouth. He sits on the porch, the wicker chair, facing the stretch of Blue Ridge woods that was infinite to me then, even though the road ran 100 meters beyond. The question feels authentic, but I can feel its danger. I stare at his hands, my chest barely higher than his lap. Even then, I know something abides in the open hands, a fullness, a thing, the answer I seek? We open our hands, something goes. What?

Sausalito eases itself within the final breath before the Headlands exhale into the Bay. We pass the storefronts designed for fat, white people. The Dippin' Dots cart is next to a rest-aurant that rests itself over the water, perched on a pier, a series of exposed wood beams disappearing into the murky water. Barnacles grow all over the wood.

See, look at that, I say. Isn't everyone freaking out about that building relying on *wood in water*? I mean, isn't it soaking, softening, rotting?

Well, yeah, I guess, says Marie.

Then, I say.

Eventually, my roommate says.

Then what? I say.

Then, they build another one that won't rot for a while, he says.

I ball my fists and shake, and let out a contained growl, only for them.

Dippin' Dots! Marie says, and runs along the pier towards the cart.

One week after we shared a bed, you looked at me from across the car that shielded you from my barbed questions. Your eyes showed that you had rubbed me off, and I disappeared from you: the mucous, the semen, the spit, the hair, the particles of me, all gone. Where did it go? If it is a gift, who have I given it to, now? Do I have any say in this?

I stare at my brick ceiling—when will it corrupt enough to give up and fall on my face while I sleep? How many shakes will it take?

We made the Titanic, we made the Hindenburg, we made the Challenger Shuttle. We made Fukushima. We make love.

I am a structure. Dust is skin, floating in the light. When we sleep, we not only shut off from the waking world, we dissipate, pieces of us leaving, rolling in the soft motion, in stillness. Air and water move around us, taking bit by bit. We stand, and we can hold up many things, and we are certain, even as the little bit and the little bit leave. How many shakes will I take? And what of the violence?

When I was small, a fierce and tight little bud of my eventual self, my grandmother swayed with the stories of every living thing. The late summer would swarm with dandelions, and when they were ready, the white fluffy seeds would take flight. The flower knew of its end, and would let go in one last grateful gesture of life, a soft woolen sigh into the air. And off the seeds would go, twilling with the air and light. I chased them, delighted when they grazed my outstretched palm, but I had no desire to fold my fist around them, and they'd take flight again. My grandmother looked off, beyond me and the seeds, over the horizon and somewhere beyond. It was a face I couldn't have understood. My father opens his hands and says nothing when I ask him why he is my father.
One last grateful gesture of the mystery, and why it should stay that way. The world breathes, in its own woven way.

We are sitting on the dock, Marie, my roommate, and I, facing the Bay on a sunny day. Below us the water, we supported by rotting beams of wood. We are nibbling our Dippin' Dots—nibbling flakes of skin, sea water, salt, early morning sneezes, fingernail crud, snot, rust, cat hair, dog dander, fly eggs, cum, pussy juice, sweat, pus, shit, fish ick, toe jam, rotten meat, fungus.

This is fucking good, my roommate says, little bits of Dots sticking to his hipster whiskers. Marie is too busy tonguing the dots to say anything at all. Yeah, it is, I say.

ACKNOWLEDGEMENTS

Essays from this collection have appeared in the following publications:

Callisto: "The Story of Every Living Thing"
Chelsea Station: "Leaving a Mark"
The Citron Review: "Make Sure to See the Exit Door"
Fifth Wednesday: "First Love: A"
Fourteen Hills: "Sunset, 2006 (The Modern Prometheus, reprise)"
Hashtag Queer Anthology: "To An Ex-Lover, After A Natural History of the Senses"
New Millennium Writings: "Growl"

Thank you to Lambda Literary and the Possums, who gave birth to this collection of essays after spending one week together, in Los Angeles, in love. And to J. K. Fowler and the Nomadic Press team for giving them a space.

To the dedicated teachers and readers of these essays in their horrific and juvenile incarnations: Toni Mirosevich, D.A. Powell, Randall Kenan, Maxine Chernoff, ZZ Packer, Robert Glück, Junse Kim, Janet Sarbanes, Kazim Ali, Peter Gadol, Douglas Kearney, Chad Koch, Ploi Pirapokin, Katrin Gibb, Kendra Schynert, Carson Beker, Jennifer Lewis, Juliana Delgado Lopera, Sarah Broderick, and Monique Mero. And thanks to Ari Moskowitz, for editing the final collection. Thanks, y'all, for helping me make (non)sense of them.

To the friends who keep me fierce. To Angela Davis, James Baldwin, Richard Rodriguez: I am gratefully in your shadow.

My mama, Peggy, for all of it.

And Mark, my yubbies, my Yubs. Yubs.

MIAH JEFFRA is from Baltimore, and the South, in general. He holds degrees from the California Institute of the Arts, San Francisco State University and Oglethorpe University. He has been awarded the New Millennium Fiction Prize, The Sidney Lanier Prize for Fiction, and the Clark- Gross Novel Award; a finalist for the Arcadia Prize in nonfiction and New Letters Fiction Prize; a Lambda Literary Fellowship in nonfiction; and residencies from Arteles, Red Gate, Ragdale, and The Hub City Writers Project. Jeffra serves as editor of *Foglifter Press*, and teaches writing, rhetoric, and cultural studies at Santa Clara University and San Francisco Art Institute. He lives in San Francisco with his husband and roommates, both human and canine. He dances every day.